Written by

Dr. Jean Feldman

Editor: Dorothy Ly
Photographs: Michael Jarret
Designer/Production: Rebekah O. Lewis
Art Director: Moonhee Pak
Project Director: Stacey Faulkner

Table of Contents

Cheers to Begin the Day

Cheers to Grab Attention

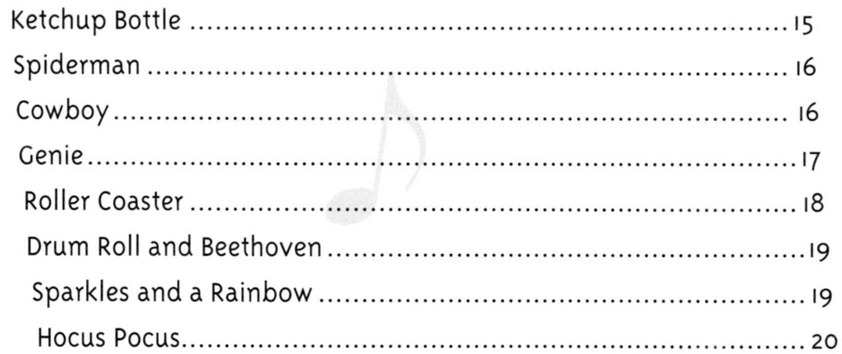

Transition Cheers

Feel Good Cheers

Celebration Cheers

Cheers to End the Day

Introduction

It's time for a cheer! It's time to feel good!
It's time to celebrate every day!

Cheer along with Dr. Jean! Cheers and attention grabbers are a natural way to develop oral language, auditory memory, and fluency that lay a foundation for learning in the classroom. This valuable book is full of fun and lively cheers designed to energize, motivate, and engage children's learning, and help them know what to expect. Incorporate a variety of cheers throughout each day. Use cheers to start the day, focus children's attention, line up students, and facilitate recall at the end of the day. These cheers will make the class smile and laugh, as they add a touch of "happy" to the day!

The cheers are organized into six categories for easy reference:

Cheers to Begin the Day—
Add these cheers to the class morning routines to begin the day with a smile!

Attention Grabbers—
When Shh! doesn't work, these chants and activities will do the trick to help settle children down and focus their attention.

Transition Cheers—
These tips will keep the day moving in a smooth and positive way.

Feel Good Cheers—
Encourage and motivate children with these fun, positive reinforcements.

Celebration Cheers—
Celebrate the big and little accomplishments throughout the day.

Cheers to End the Day—
It's important to start the day with a smile and also end the day with a smile!

Included in this book you'll find:

- Photos that model the step-by-step movements for the majority of the cheers
- Simple, easy-to-follow written directions on how to perform each cheer
- Hints, suggestions, and variations for select cheers

Brain-based research suggests that activities such as cheers can be helpful in preparing students to learn. Rather than immediately diving into content, you may find it more productive to instead use the first few minutes of class time to allow students to express and redirect their feelings. By employing various emotional processing activities, you can steer students' emotions in a positive direction that is conducive to learning. Such activities—which include walks, humor, partner time, positive social rituals, celebrations, reflection, sharing, or physical activities—can often find their expression in cheers. By using the energizing and motivational cheers, you will be able to reach students before you teach them.

Getting Started

Why Use Cheers?

One of our most important responsibilities as educators is to help children recognize who they are and what they can do. The cheers featured in this book can help students feel unique and special. There are many benefits to using cheers with your students. Cheers can aid students' social development and learning in the following ways:

- Provide a "brain break" by sending blood and oxygen to the brain
- Build connections between the brain's two hemispheres as movements cross the body's midline
- Facilitate language development
- Develop eye-hand coordination
- Nurture social skills as all students participate together
- Reduce discipline problems by redirecting children in positive ways
- Engage children and focus their attention
- Relieve stress and frustration through clapping and cheering

How to Use Cheers in Your Classroom?

Adapt cheers to the age level and interests of your students. Try the cheers out with the class and see which ones students like best. Also, encourage students to make up their own cheers for the class. Remember, if there's laughing and smiling, it shows that children are having fun and have caught the enthusiasm to participate in classroom learning!

Choose one cheer each day to introduce to the class. Perform the new cheer throughout the day, and then save and share all the learned cheers by using some of the ideas suggested below:

- As new cheers are taught to students, write them on star shapes and display them in the classroom.
- Write cheers on sentence strips. Allow one child be the "cheerleader" each day and choose the cheers that he or she likes best. Put those cheers in a pocket chart, and do them during appropriate moments throughout the day.
- Write the name of the cheers on craft sticks, and put them in a can. Let children take turns choosing cheers for the class to do.
- Make copies of the cheers, and save them in a Cheerios box or Cheer detergent box. Let children pick cheers out of the box.
- Send home copies of cheers so children and parents can do them together at home.

Four "H" Hello

Cut out the numeral 5, a heart, a hand, and a pair of lips from 8½" x 11" pieces of felt or fun foam, and place them on the floor. Have children stand on the symbol for how they would like to be greeted.

1. If they stand on the 5, give them high fives.
2. If they stand on the heart, give them hugs.
3. If they stand on the hand, give them handshakes.
4. If they stand on the lips, give them "Hollywood kisses" by pretending to kiss the air to the right and left of the child's head.

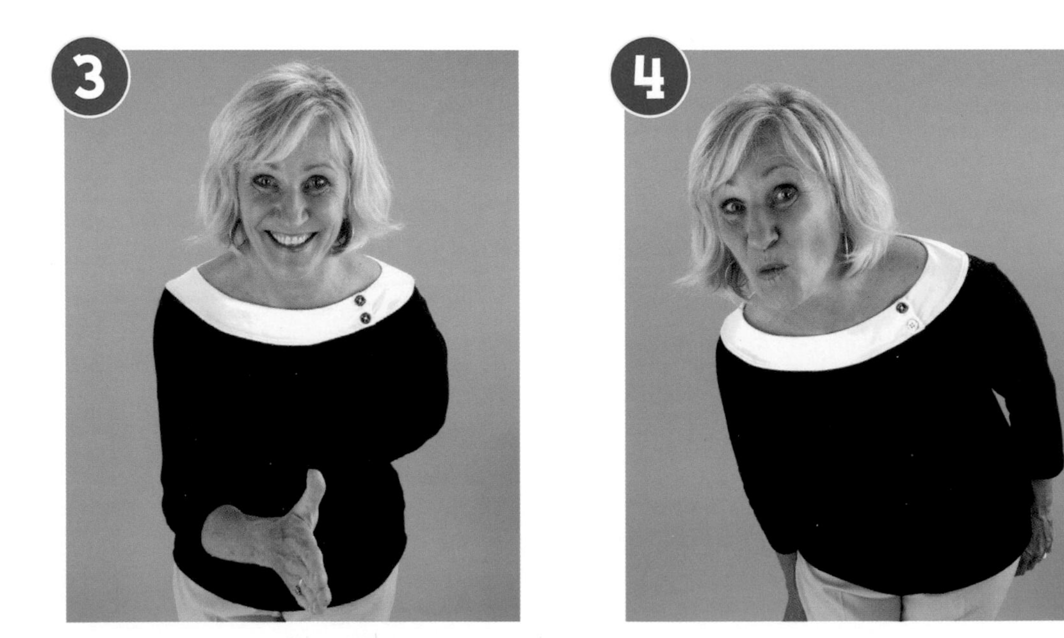

H-A-P-P-Y

1 Say, *Is everybody happy?*

2 Have children respond, *Yes, ma'am (or sir)!*

3 Together, spell and clap on each letter, *H-a-p-p-y.*

4 Loudly say, *Happy* all together.

When having students line up, say, ***Is everybody ready?***
Have students respond, ***Yes, ma'am (or sir)! R-e-a-d-y! Ready!***

Morning Rock

1. Begin this beat by slowly stomping one foot two times.
2. Then clap once. Use the children's names and chant to the beat:

    Stomp, stomp, clap. Stomp, stomp, clap. Then say,

    We think (first child's name) *is super.*

    We think (second child's name) *is super.*

    We think (third child's name) *is super.*

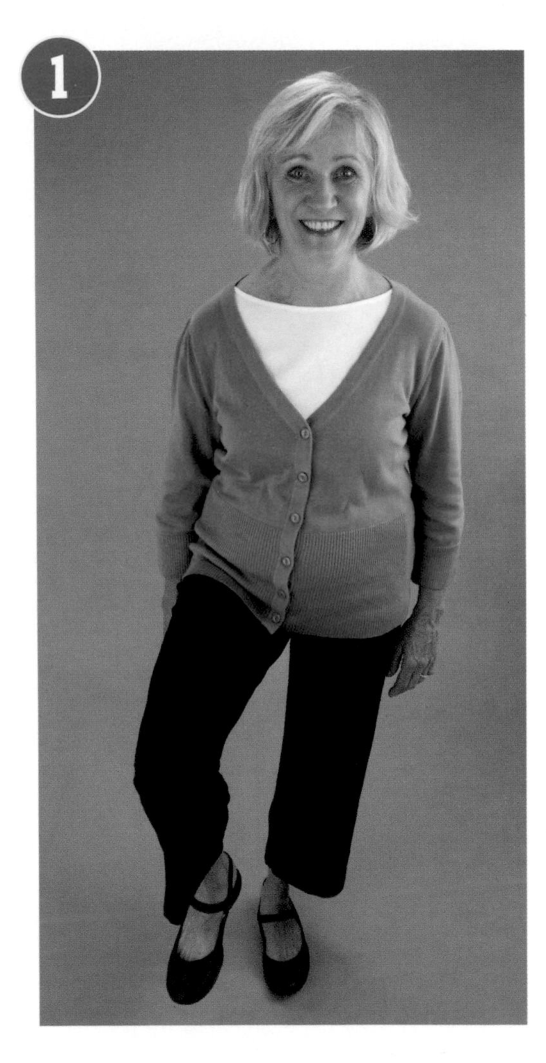

Thumb Kiss

1. Have children hold up their right thumbs.
2. Go around the room and touch your right thumb to students' right thumbs. Make a smacking noise in the air when the thumbs touch.

Starting Lineup

1. Direct children to form two lines facing each other.
2. Call out each child's name, and say something positive about each child.
3. Have each child run between the two lines as the other classmates give him or her high fives and pats on the back.

This is a great activity on "test" day.

Three Cheers

1. In a loud voice, say, *Give me cheer number one!* (Have children cheer loudly with *Yea!*)
2. In a softer voice, say, *Give me cheer number two!* (Have children cheer *Yea!* more quietly.)
3. In a whisper, say, *Give me cheer number three!* (Have children do a silent cheer by waving their arms above their head and smiling.)

Make Rain

1. Say, *Let's make rain. Do what I do.*
   Tap right index finger on left palm.
   Tap index finger and middle fingers.
   Tap index, middle, and ring fingers.
   Tap index, middle, ring, and pinky fingers.
2. Clap hands together loudly.
3. Continue claping hands and then stomp feet.
4. Reverse the motions.
   Stop stomping and just clap hands.
   Tap index, middle, ring, and pinky fingers on palm.
   Tap index, middle, and ring fingers.
   Tap index and middle fingers.
   Tap index finger on palm.
5. End the activity by slowly bringing palms together and putting them quietly down onto the lap.

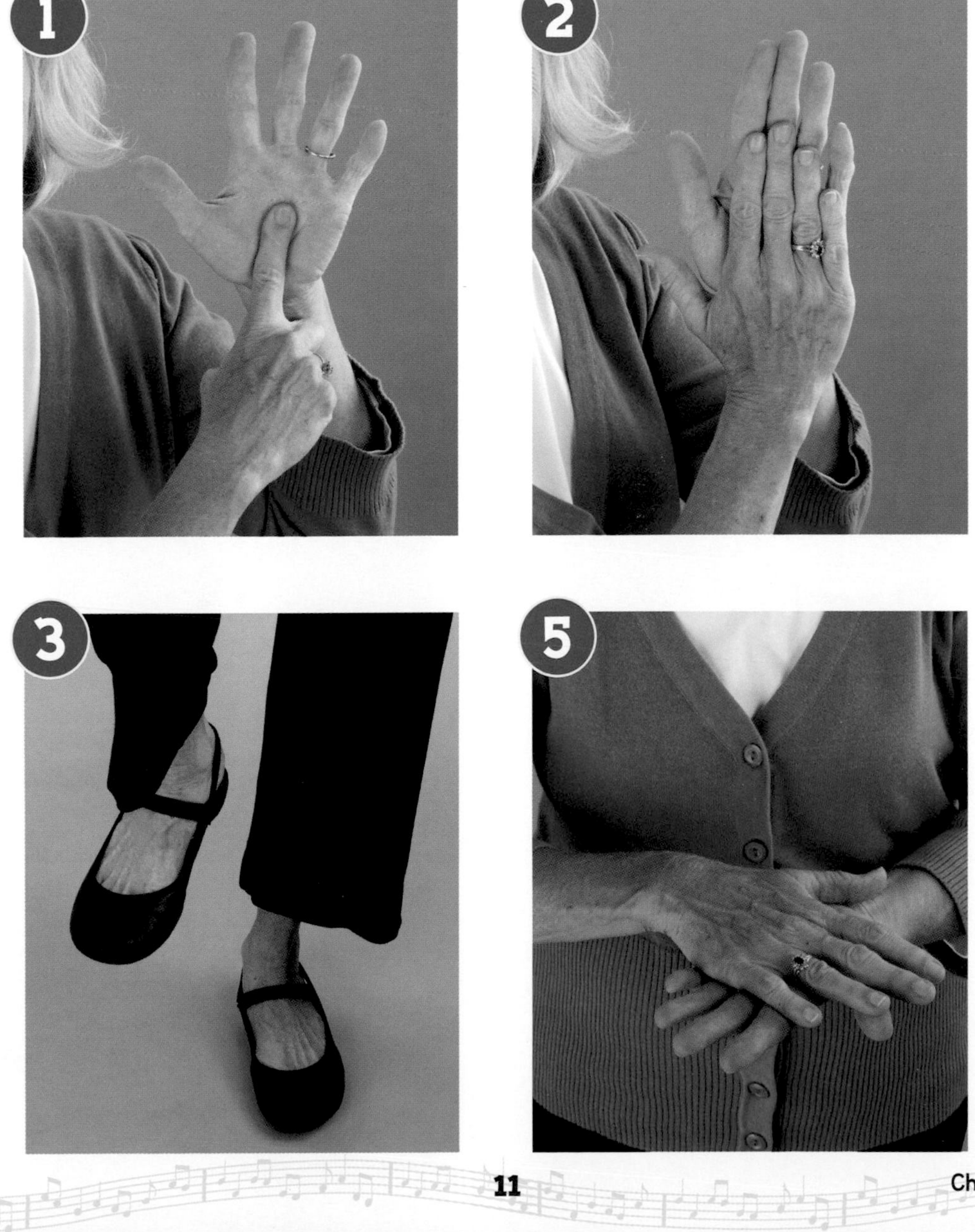

Sprinkler

Put the left hand on the back of the head.

Stick the right arm out in front and begin to sweep arm across the body.

Make a *Shh! Shh! Shh!* sound while jerking the right arm in front like a rotating sprinkler.

Pizza

1. Put right palm on top of left palm and say, *Here is our pizza.*
2. Say, *Make a pizza, make a pizza,* while clapping left hand on top of right hand and then right hand on top of left hand.
3. Pretend to take a bite and stretch some cheese from the mouth and say, *Cheesiola!*
4. Hold up the right palm as if holding a pizza in the air and say, *Mama Mia!*

Bubblegum

1. Pretend to unwrap a piece of gum and put it in the mouth.
2. Dramatically pretend to chew and move head from side to side.
3. Cup hands near the mouth and gradually move them a little farther apart while pretending to blow a bubble.
4. Pause. Then clap hands and say, *Pop!*

Rattlesnake

1. Place both palms together in front of the body and wiggle hands left and right in a forward direction.
2. Thrust hands directly in front of you. Make a hissing sound and quickly stick tongue in and out like a snake.

Ketchup Bottle

Hold up a fist and say, *Show me your ketchup bottle.*

Pound on your fist with other hand as if thumping a bottle.

As a variation for a mustard bottle, pretend to squeeze the bottle and blow through mouth to make the sound of air blowing in and out of the bottle.

1. Put hands out, palms up, and bend middle and ring fingers down.
2. Move hands from side to side as if throwing a web, and say, *Ssss!*

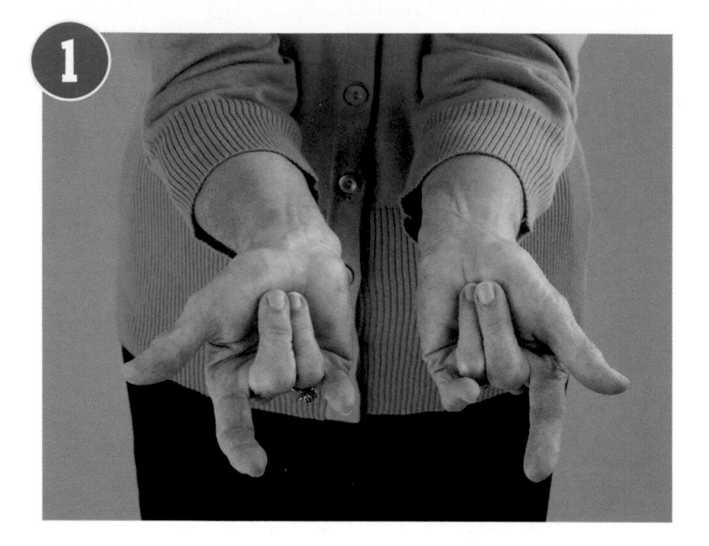

1. Put left hand on left hip and raise right hand with the index finger in the air and say, *Yee*.
2. Circle the right index finger around like a lasso and lean back as you say, *haw!*

Genie

1. Fold arms on top of one another like a genie.
2. Raise forearms. Then fold them back down as shown in step 1.
3. Stretch forearms out in front. Then fold them back as shown in step 1. Continue to raise forearms, and fold, stretch out forearms, and fold faster and faster.

Roller Coaster

Tell students to hold on to the roller coaster.

Make a clicking noise with tongue and slowly raise arms up in increments until they are above the head.

Pause for a second and then say, *Woo!*

Swoop hands down and then up again like riding a roller coaster.

Drum Roll and Beethoven

1. Say, *Give me a drum roll.* (Have children gently tap their fingers on their desks or thighs.)
2. Say, *Where is Beethoven?* (Have children pretend to strum a bass back and forth as they hum the opening notes of Beethoven's Fifth Symphony, *Da, da, da, daaa. Da, da, da, daaa!*)

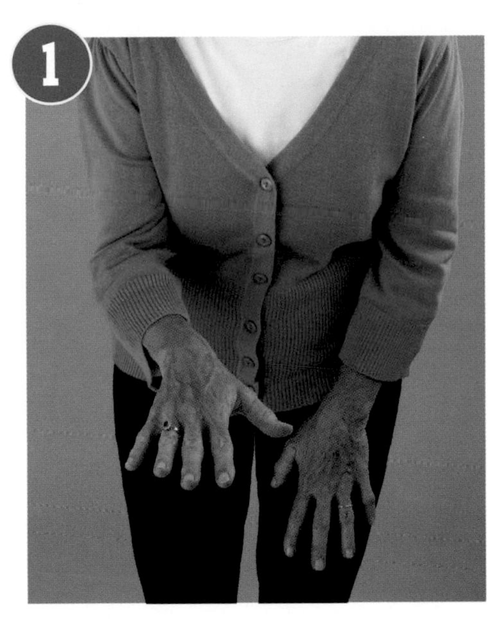

Sparkles and a Rainbow

1. Say, *Sparkles!* (Hold up hands and wiggle fingers back and forth.)
2. Say, *And a rainbow.* (Open palms and move them up and around in an arch like a rainbow.)

Hocus Pocus

1. Pretend to hold a magic wand with the right hand, circle it around in front of your body, and say, *Hocus pocus!*
2. Have children touch their thumbs to their index fingers and then hold their "spectacles" up to their eyes as they reply, *Everybody focus!*

Line Up Cadence

1. Slap thighs, march, and chant:
   Lining up is easy to do
   (Have children repeat each line.)
   When you take care of only you.
2. *Feet together, hands by sides*
   We've got spirit We've got pride.
   (Point both thumbs at chest.)
3. *Sound off! 1, 2, 3, 4, at the door!*
   (Hold up each finger as you count.)
4. *Hit it again! 1, 2, 3, 4, out the door!*
   (Point one thumb back over the shoulder.)

Have a Seat

Sing this song to the tune of "Shortenin' Bread" to have children sit down on the floor with hands clasped in their laps:

Everybody have a seat, have a seat, have a seat.
Everybody have a seat on the floor.
Not on the ceiling, not on the door.
Everybody have a seat on the floor!

When you want the children to sit in chairs, sing:
Everybody have a seat, have a seat, have a seat.
Everybody have a seat on your chair.
Not on the ceiling, not in the air.
Everybody have a seat on your chair.

All Set?

1. Say, *All set?* (Snap fingers twice.) Have children respond, *You bet!* (Snap fingers twice.)

If the children are not ready, they say, ***Not yet.*** Keep repeating, ***All set?*** until the whole class responds, ***You bet!***

Hips and Lips

1. When lined up and before leaving the classroom, say, *Hips and lips* before leaving the classroom. Have children put one hand on their hips.
2. Have children put the other hand on their lips.

Say, ***Lick 'em and stick 'em.*** Children pretend to lick hands and glue them to their bodies.

Sit Down Chant

1. Use this rhythm to get children sitting quietly: Say, *Clap your hands* (clap hands 3 times). Say, *Stomp your feet* (stomp feet 3 times).
2. Quietly say: *Put your b*

Line Up Poem

Have children recite this poem before leaving the classroom:

I'm looking straight ahead of me.
My arms are at my side.
My feet are quiet as can be.
I'm ready to go outside.

To help children keep their hands to themselves, demonstrate how to make "butterfly wings" by putting your hands behind your back and sticking out your elbows.

Kiss Your Brain!

1. When children answer a question or say something clever, say, *Kiss your brain!* (Kiss fingertips).
2. Then touch fingertips on the child's head.

Kiss Your Heart!

1. When children do something kind, say, *Kiss your heart!*
2. Have children kiss their own fingertips and place them on their chest.

Smiley

1. Say, *Let's give ourselves a smiley.* Point to each eye, and make a clicking sound with tongue at each point.
2. Then have children pretend to draw a big curved smile on their faces. When you complete the smile, say, *Ching!*

Cheese and Grater

1. Hold up your left palm. Say, *Here is the grater.*
2. Hold up your right fist. Say, *Here is the cheese.*
3. Pretend to scrape the cheese on the grater, and say, *You're great, great, great!*

Shine Your Halo

1. Move right palm above the head in a circular motion, and say, *Shine your halos.*
2. Tell children, *You are my angels!*

Say, ***Fluff your wings,*** and have children pretend to fluff their wings above their shoulders.

Looking Good!

1. Use two index fingers to draw an invisible mirror frame in front of body. Make a clicking sound with tongue where each side of the frame ends.
2. Fluff hair as if primping and say, *Looking good!*

Use children's individual names in this cheer. For example, ***Looking good, Jana!*** or ***Looking good, Carlos***

AWESOME!

Clap hands on each letter as you spell, *A –W – E* (pause) *S- O – M – E.*

Put out left palm and say, *Awesome!*

Put out right palm and say, *Awesome!*

Put hands on hips, wiggle body, and say, *Totally!*

Pencil Sharpener

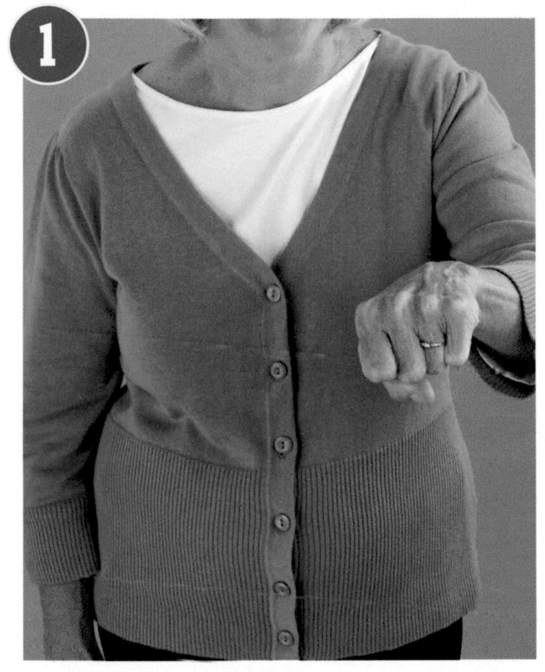

Put left fist in front and say, *Here is your pencil sharpener.*

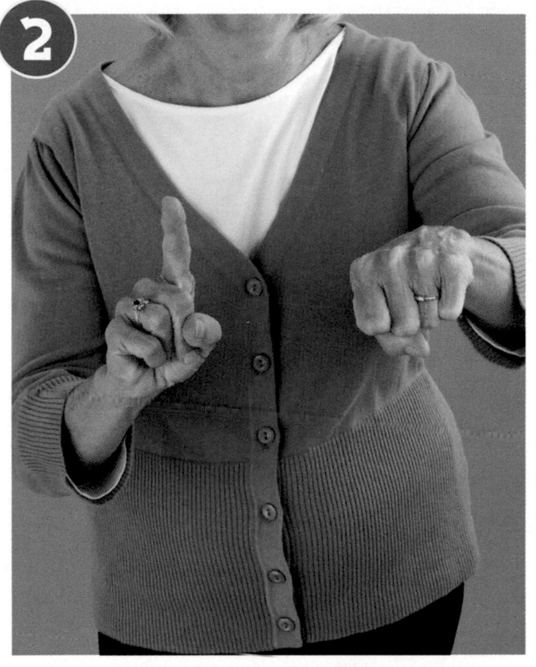

Hold up right index finger and say, *Here is your pencil.*

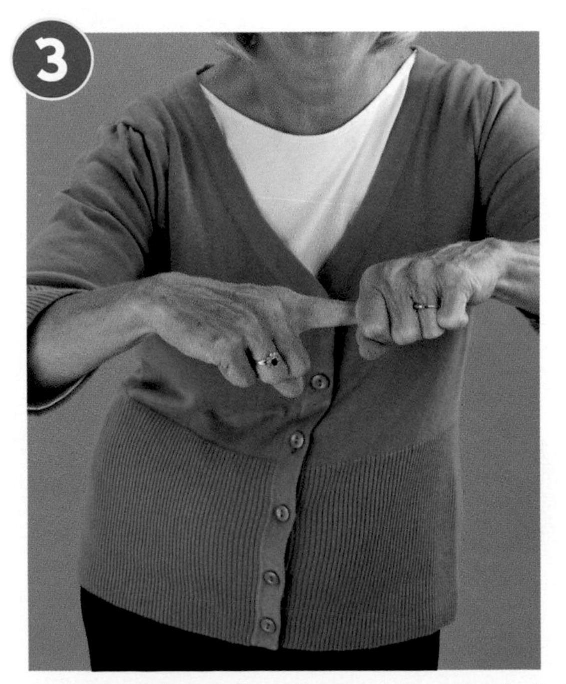

Insert right index finger into the left fist and say, *Buzz!*

Remove the index finger, pretend to blow off shavings, and then point to the child and say, *You're sharp!*

Go Bananas!

1. Say, *Peel to the left.* (Step left and put out left hand.)
2. Say, *Peel to the right.* (Step to the right and put out right hand.)
3. Say, *Peel down the middle.* (Lean forward and put out both hands.)
4. Say, *And take a bite!* (Open mouth and bite.)
5. Say, *Go bananas!* (Jump around and wiggle.)

Seal of Approval

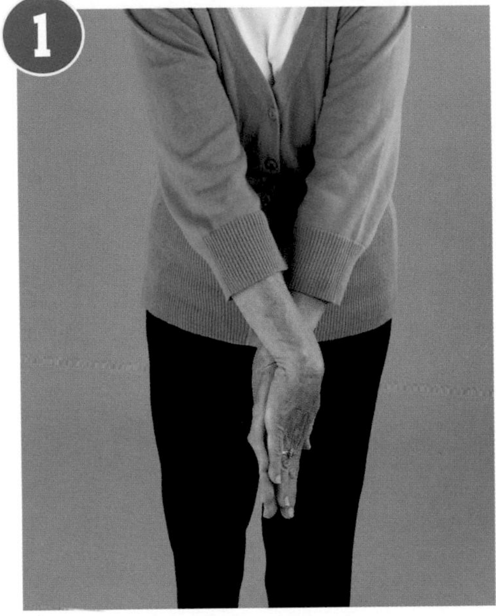

Stretch out arms in front crossing one over the other and placing both palms together.

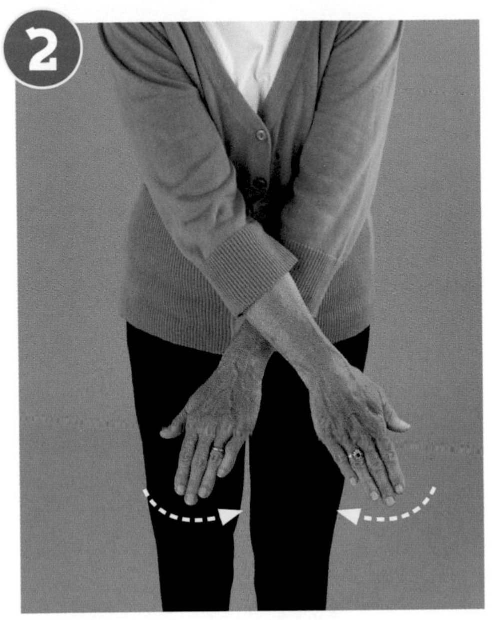

Clap hands and pretend to bark like a seal. Say, *Arf! Arf! Arf!*

Lobster Clap

Extend and hold fingers close together and stick out thumbs.

Open and close fingers and thumbs like pincers on a lobster.

Fantastic

1. Say, *Get out your spray bottle.* (Hold out right fist.)
2. Open and close fingers three times as if squirting a bottle and say, *Psssh! Psssh! Psssh!*
3. Wave left palm in a circular motion as if wiping and say, FANTASTIC!

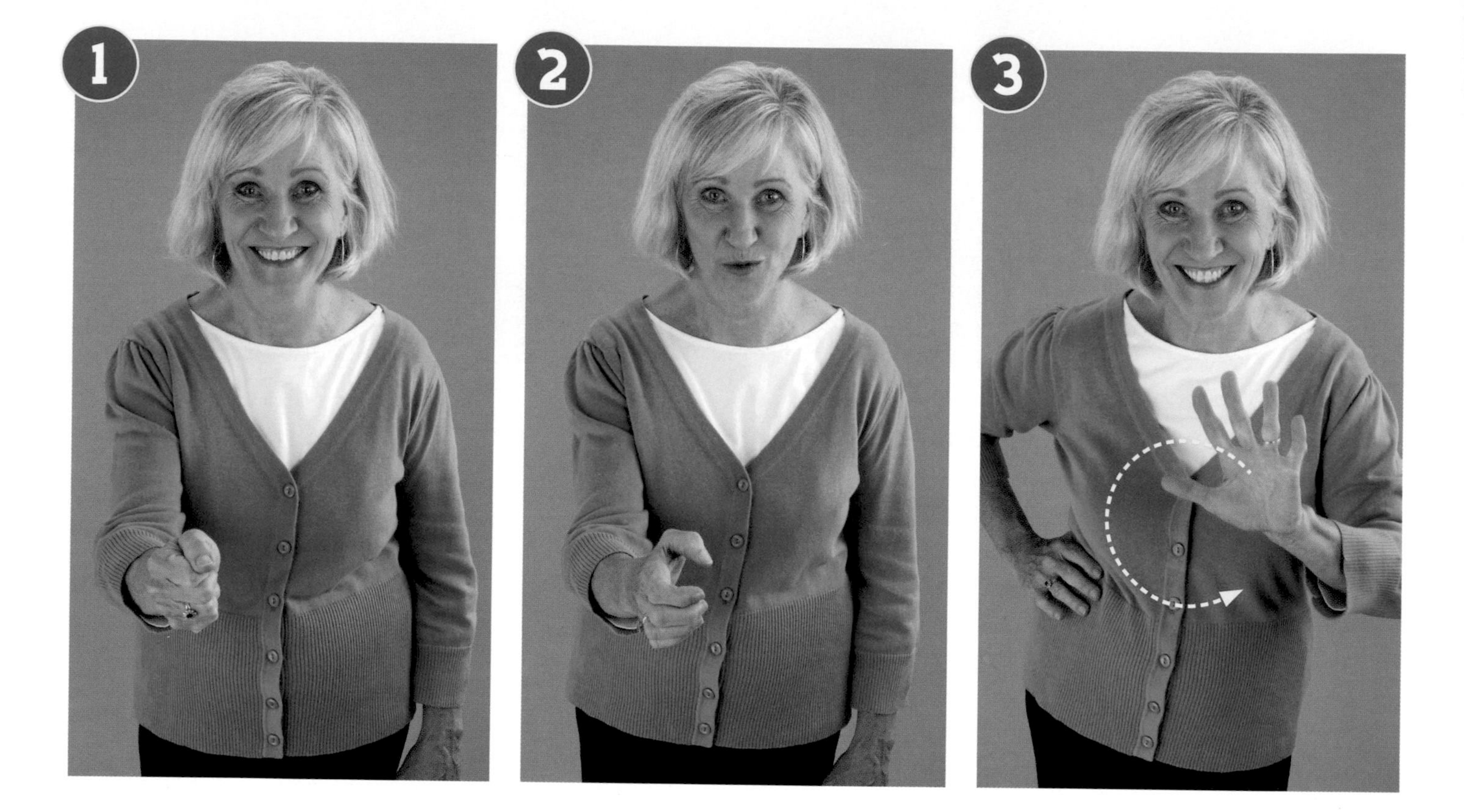

How Does My Teacher Feel about Me?

1. Say, *How does my teacher feel about me?*
2. Have children say, *I'm as special as special can be, because my teacher believes in me!*

Hamburger

1. Say, *Show me your hamburger* and pat hands pretending to make a meat patty.
2. Say, *Put it on the grill.* Hold out right hand and wiggle it and say, *Sssss!*
3. Say, *Is it done yet?* Turn over right hand and say, *Not yet!*
4. Hold out right hand again and wiggle it and say, *Sssss!* Turn hand over and say, *Is it done yet?*
5. Stick up right thumb, and pull hand back toward the body and say, *Well done!*

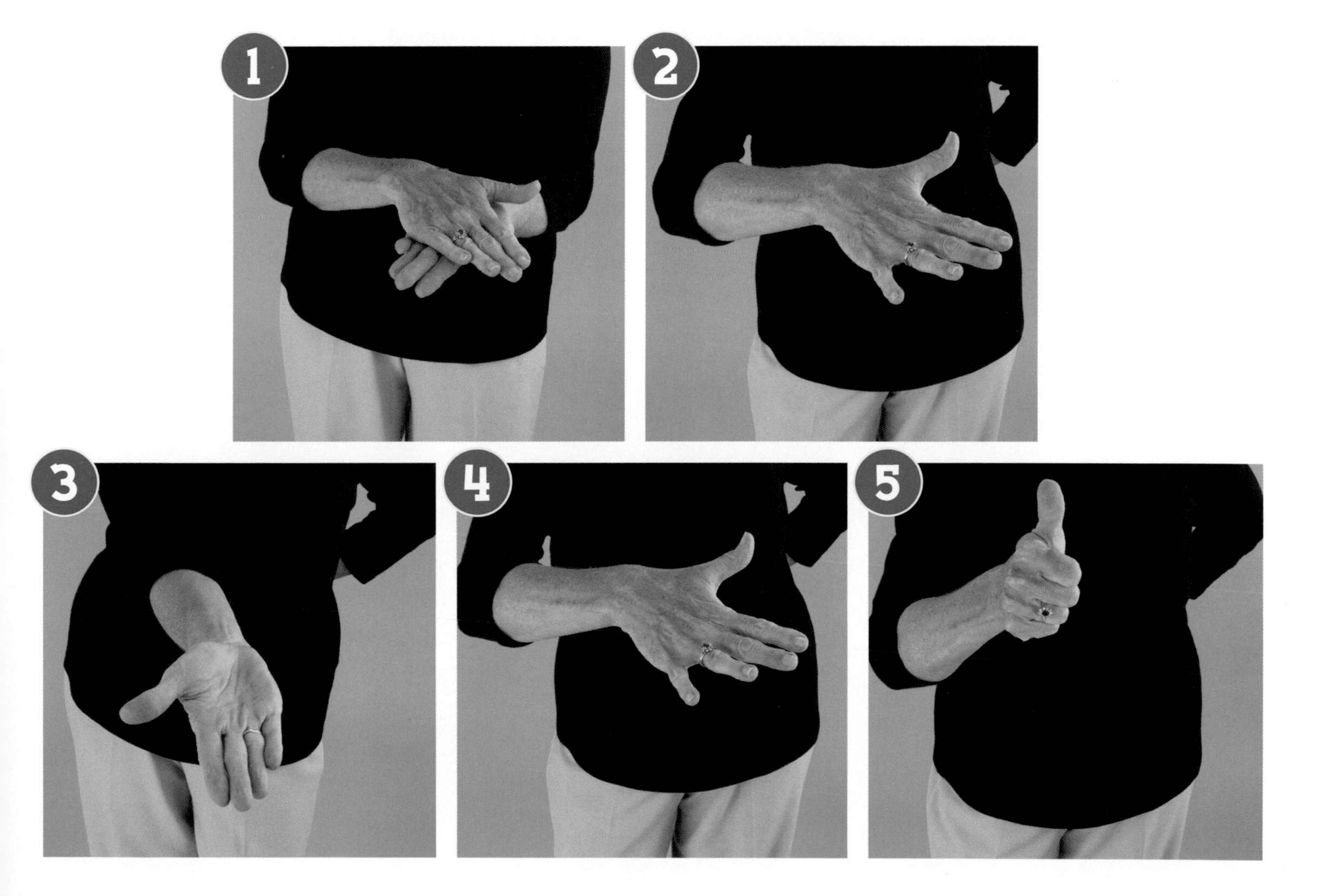

X-cellent!

1. Raise fists in the air.
2. Cross forearms to make an X. Say, *Excellent!*

WOW!

1. Make W's with hands by spreading index, middle, and ring fingers.
2. Open mouth wide to make a letter (O). Place the W's on each side of the mouth to make the word, *WOW!*

Turn the W's upside down to make the word *MOM!* Make a C with the right hand and an L with the left hand. Open eyes wide and place the letters by eyes to spell *COOL.*

Parrot

1. Bend elbows and put hands under armpits to make wings.
2. Flap elbows, squawk, and say, *Aawk! You did a good job! Aawk! You did a good job!*

Donkey

1. Stand on right foot with elbows bent and fists in the air like a bucking donkey.
2. Bend back at the waist slightly, rocking back and forth. Have the girls say for the boys, *Hee-haw! Hee-haw! He always does a good job!* Have the boys say for the girls, *She-haw! She-haw! She always does a good job!*

Pirate

1. Cover up one eye with palm and say, *Put on your eye patch.*
2. Say, *Arrrgh!* out of the corner of the mouth. Then say, *Way to go, matey!*

That's the Way I Like It

1. Slide hands back and forth to the left and say, *That's the way, uh-huh, uh-huh, I like it.*
2. Slide hands back and forth to the right and say, *That's the way, uh-huh, uh-huh, I like it.* Repeat.

Trucker

Say, *Show me your steering wheel*, and pretend to grab a steering wheel.

Make an *Rrrrr* sound while pretending to turn the wheel and drive.

Hold up the right hand, pretend to pull on a horn, and say, *Honk! Honk!*

Put the left hand near the mouth like it is a CB radio microphone and say, *Good job, good buddy!*

Standing Ovation

1. Have children stand.
2. Hold bent arms above the head with both fingertips touching to make a circle to represent the initial O in ovation.

Hip! Hip! Hooray

Put right hand on the right hip and say, *Hip!*

Put left hand on the left hip and say, *Hip!*

Raise both hands up in the air and shout, *Hooray!*

For a variation, The teacher says, ***Hip! Hip!*** and the children shout, ***Hooray!*** as they raise their hands up in the air.

Pat Yourself on the Back

1. Stretch right arm across the chest and say, *Give yourself a pat on the back!*
2. Then reach to pat the left shoulder.

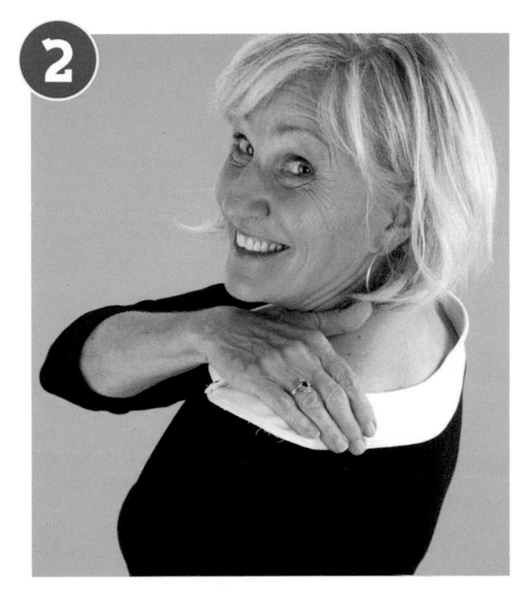

Have children pat a friend on the back and tell him or her that he or she did a good job.

Ole!

1. Put right index finger in the air. Turn body in a circle, twirl the index finger around, and say, *Ole! Ole! Ole!*
2. Throw the right hand in the air and shout, *Hey!*

Firecracker

Hold both palms together, rub them back and forth and make a sizzling sound, *Ssssss!*

Move clasped hands up in the air like a firecracker going up.

Clap hands above the head like a firecracker popping.

Wiggle fingers around and down, and say, *Ahhhh!* like people watching fireworks might do.

Disco

1. Raise right arm across the body to the left with the right index finger pointing in the air and the left hand on the left hip.
2. Then bring right arm back across the body and point finger down. As you repeat this up-and-down movement, say (to the tune of "Stayin' Alive"), *Ah, ah, ah, ah, you did a good job! You did a good job!* Repeat.

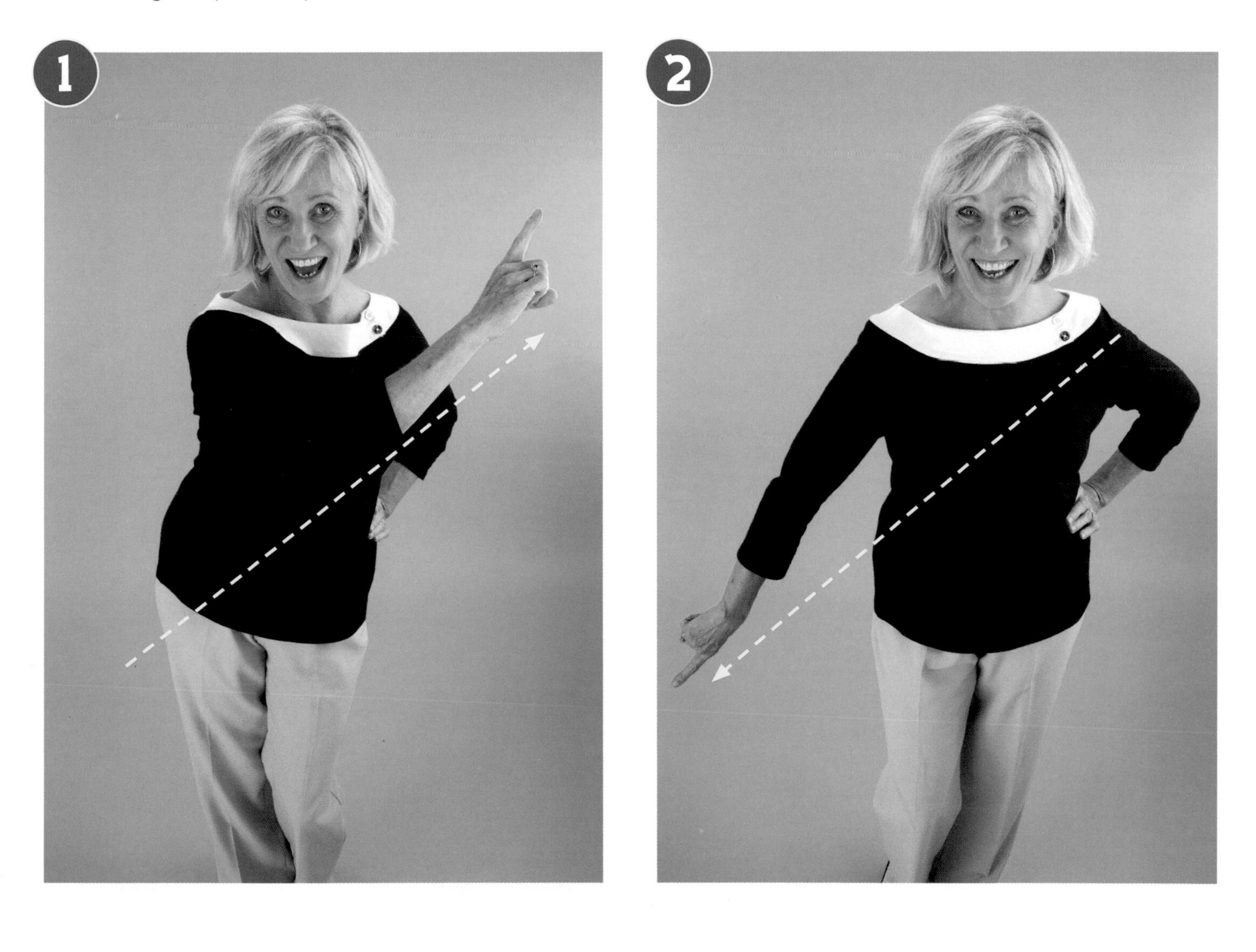

Round of Applause

Do a "round of applause" by clapping hands and moving them in a circular motion.

As a vatiation, do a "square of applause," "triangle of applause," or applause in other shapes.

High Five

Hold up the left palm and say, *Here's your FIVE.*

Wave the fingers of the right hand at the left palm as you say, *Hi FIVE!*

You can also give yourself a high five by extending your right hand in the air above your head and then slapping it with your left hand.

Clap and a Half

1. Say, *Give yourself a clap.* (Have children clap their hands.)
2. Say, *And a half.* (Have children clap with only the edge of the right hand and the palm of the left hand.)

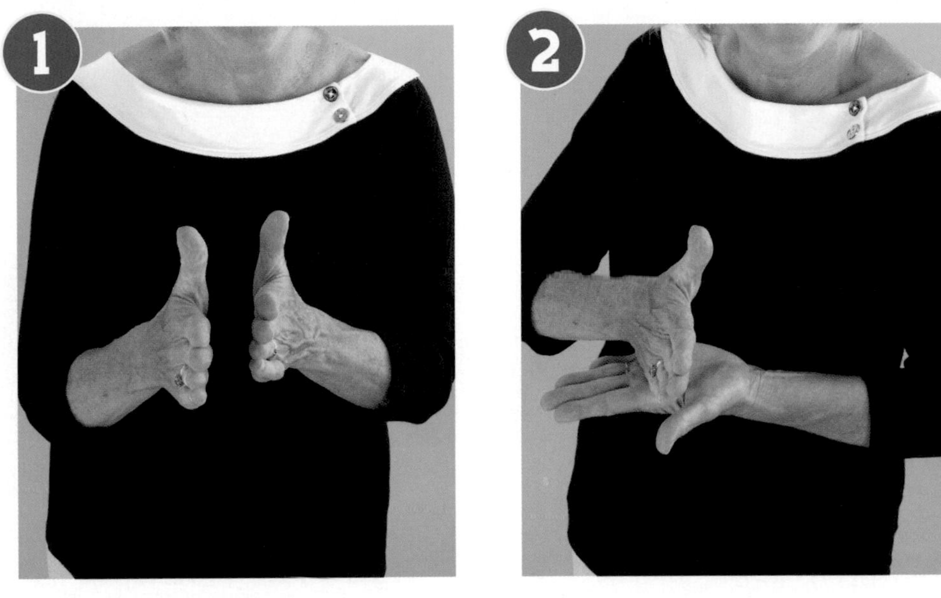

Raise the Roof

1. Push both palms up in the air and say, *This class is so awesome, let's raise the roof!*
2. Push palms out to sides and say, *Widen the walls.*
3. Push palms downward and say, *And lower the floor!*

Gold Star Class

Say, *Show me your box of gold stars,* and then hold out left palm.

Take the index finger on the right hand and touch it to the left palm as you say, *Get a gold star.*

Have children pretend to lick the tip of the finger.

Then have them touch their own foreheads and say, *We're all gold star kids!*

Remind children to just pretend to lick the star.

School Cheer

1. Say, *Give me a* (school's name) *cheer.* Have students raise their arms in the air and wiggle their fingers. (This is also the way you "applaud" in sign language.)
2. Say, *Give me a* (school's name) *yell.* Have the children do a silent yell by opening their mouths and waving their arms back and forth.

This cheer can be called a kindergarten cheer, first grade cheer, Mrs. Jones's cheer, etc.

Catch a Star Before You Go Home

1. Ask the children to think of something kind they did, something new they learned, or something that made them feel proud. Have children reach up, stretch their hands up in the air, and pretend to grab a star.
2. Then have the children put the star in their hearts (place hand over heart).

Car Wash

Have children form two lines about two feet apart. Demonstrate how to hold up palms and move them in a circular motion and say, *This is the "car wash."*

Choose one child at a time to walk through the car wash as his/her friends gently pat the child on the shoulders and make positive comments.

"Micro" Wave

Tell the children to give a "micro" wave before they leave at the end of the day.

Demonstrate by holding up right pinky finger and wiggling.

The "micro" wave is a quiet way to greet friends, siblings, the principal, and others around the school grounds.

It Is Time to Say Good-Bye

1. Begin clapping hands and stomping one foot to set the tempo. Sing these lines to the tune of "She'll Be Coming Round the Mountain".

   It is time to say good-bye to all my friends.
   It is time to say good-bye to all my friends.
   It is time to say good-bye.

2. *Give a smile and wink your eye.*
   (Smile and wink.)
   It is time to say good-bye to all my friends.

3. Say, *Good-bye friends.* (Wave and smile.)

NOTES